GRAYSCALE COLORING BOOK FOR ADULTS:

CUTE ANIMALS

Copyright © 2020 GRAYSCALE COLORING

All Rights Reserved.

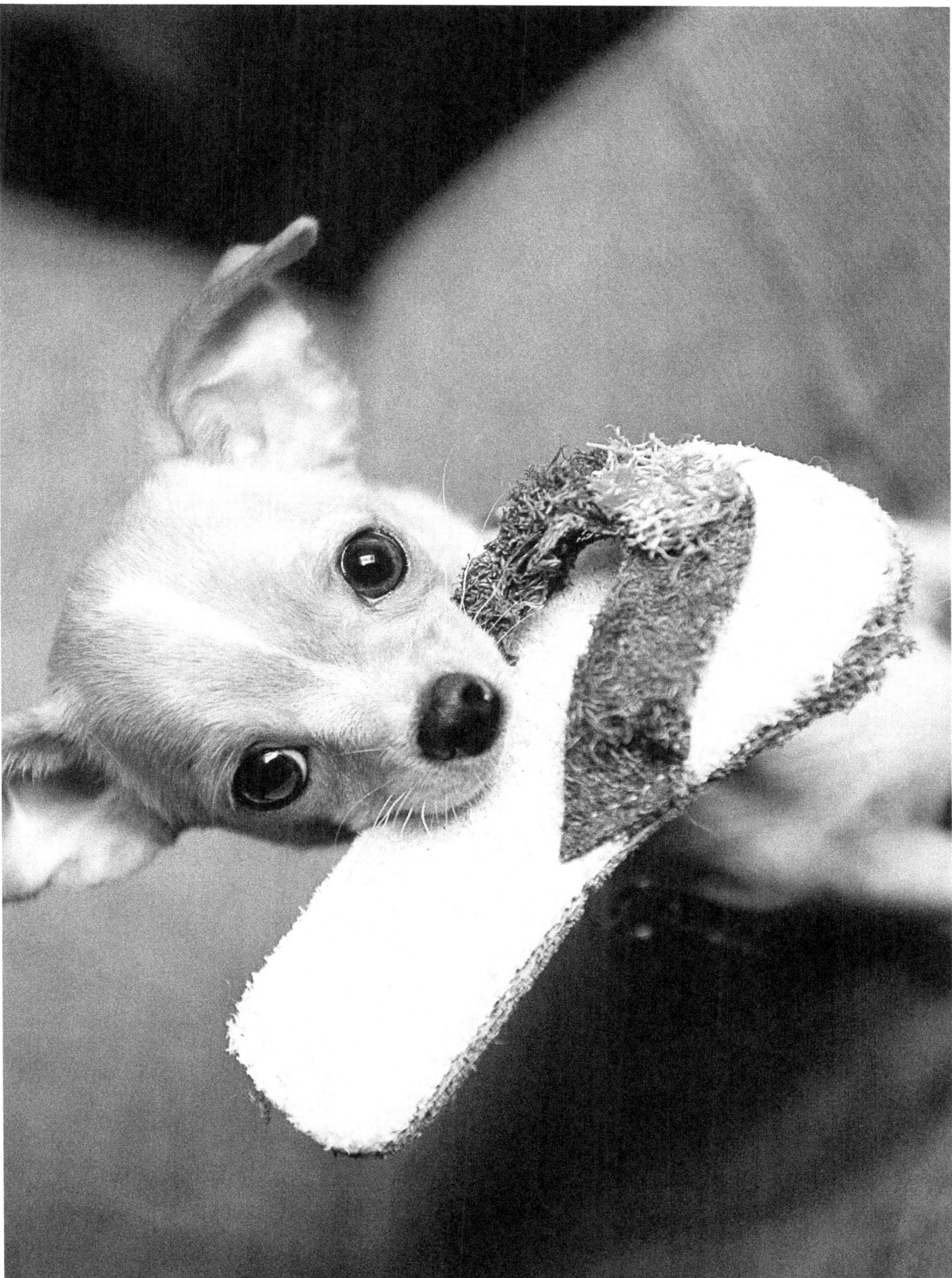

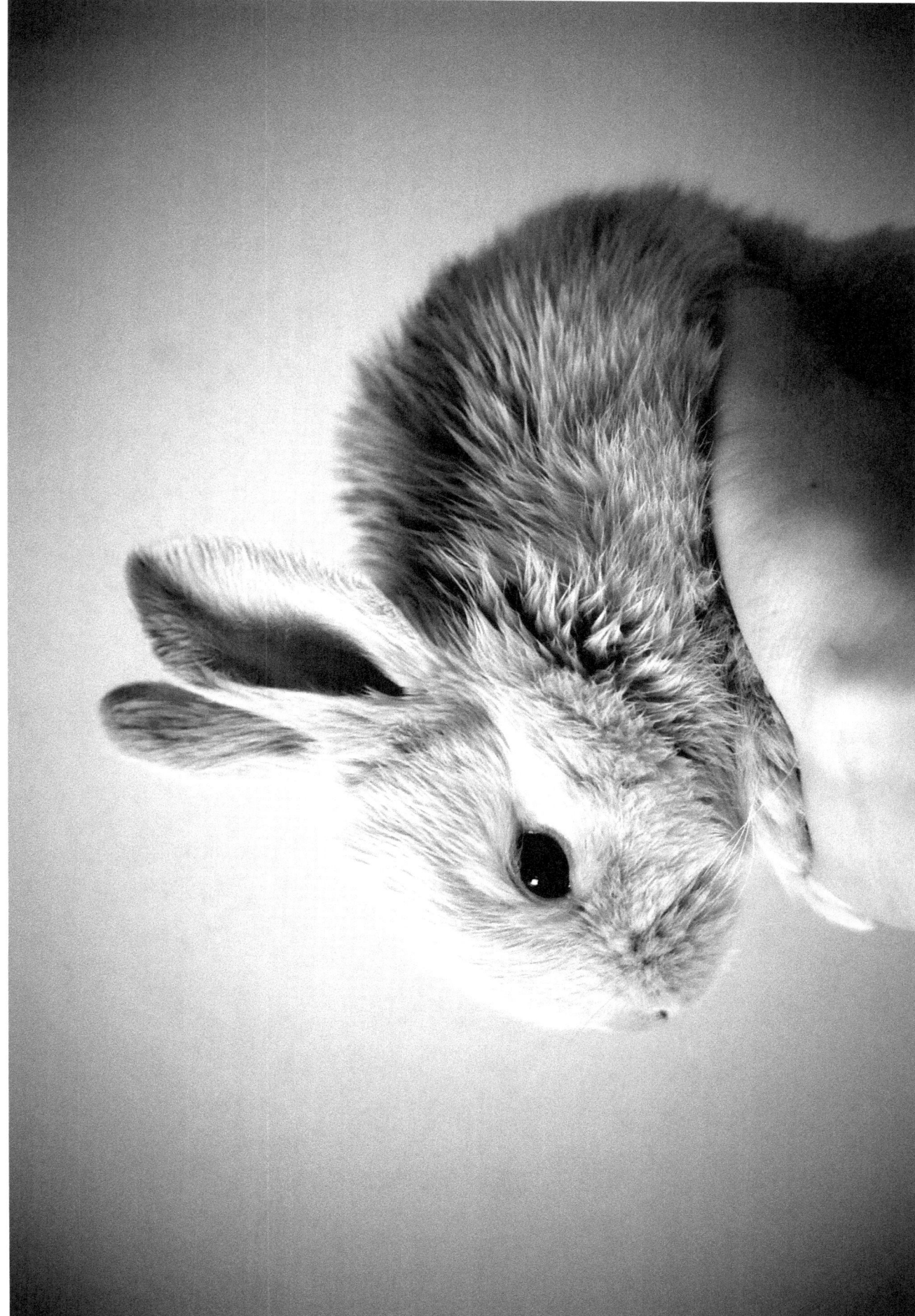

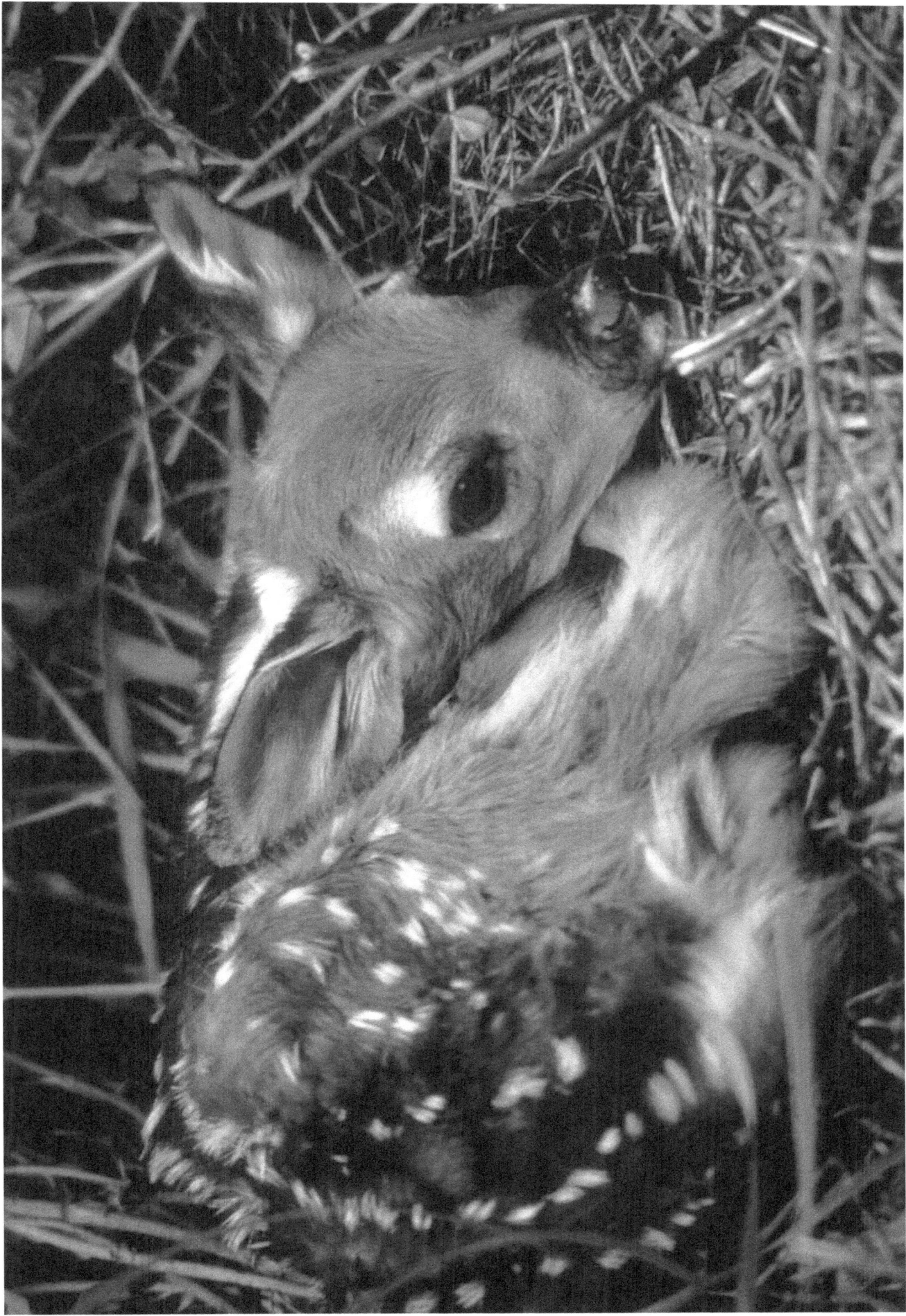

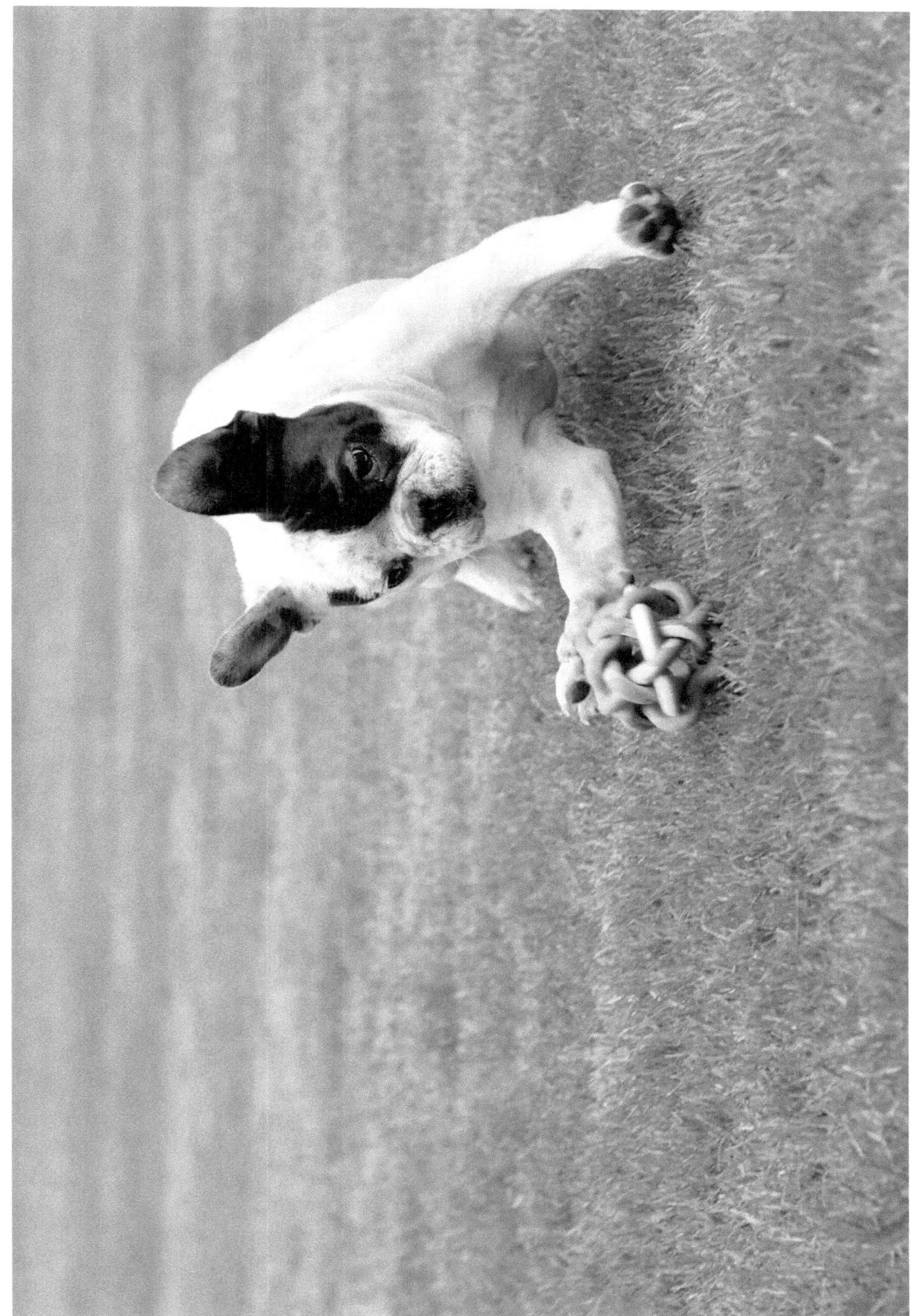

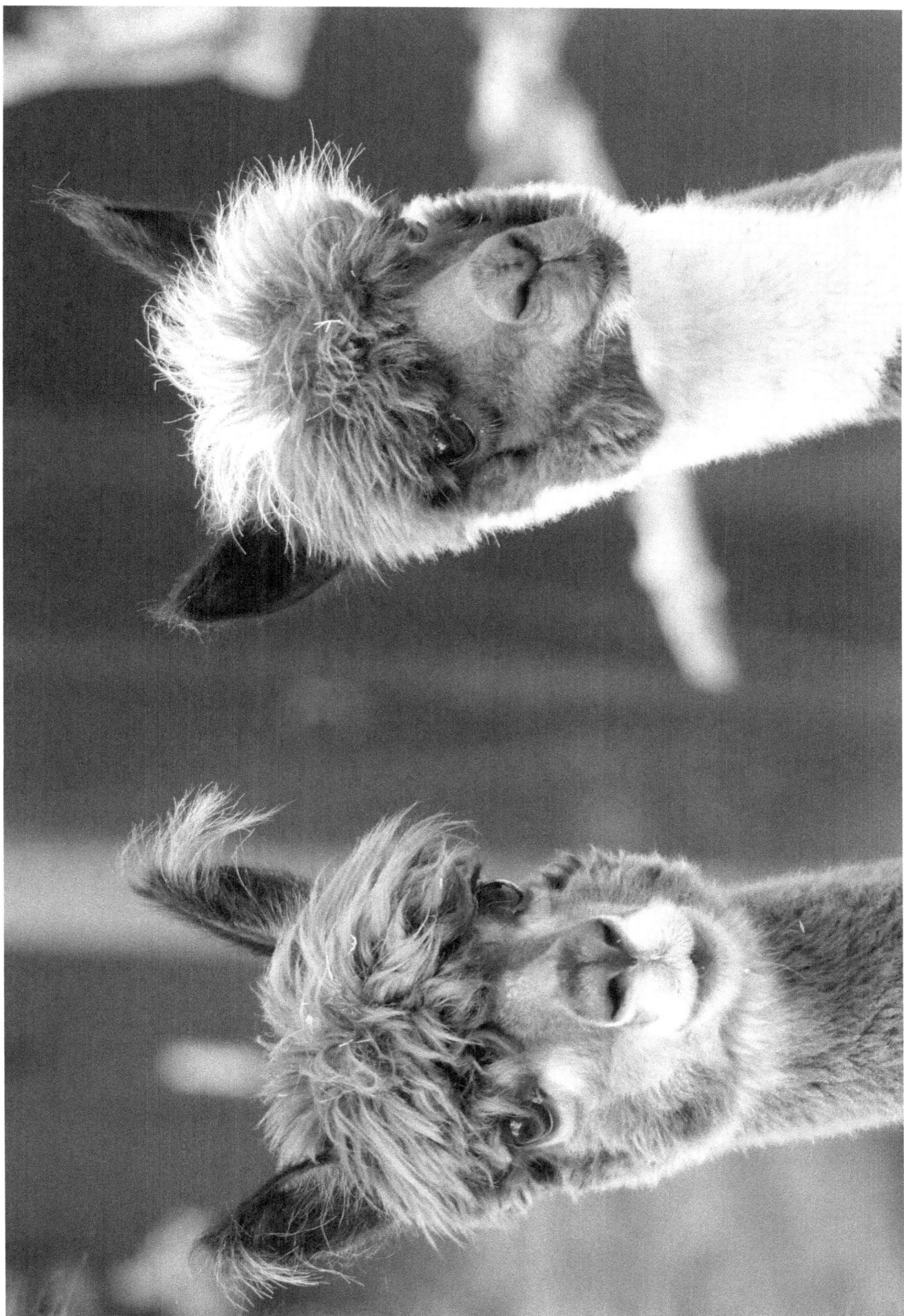

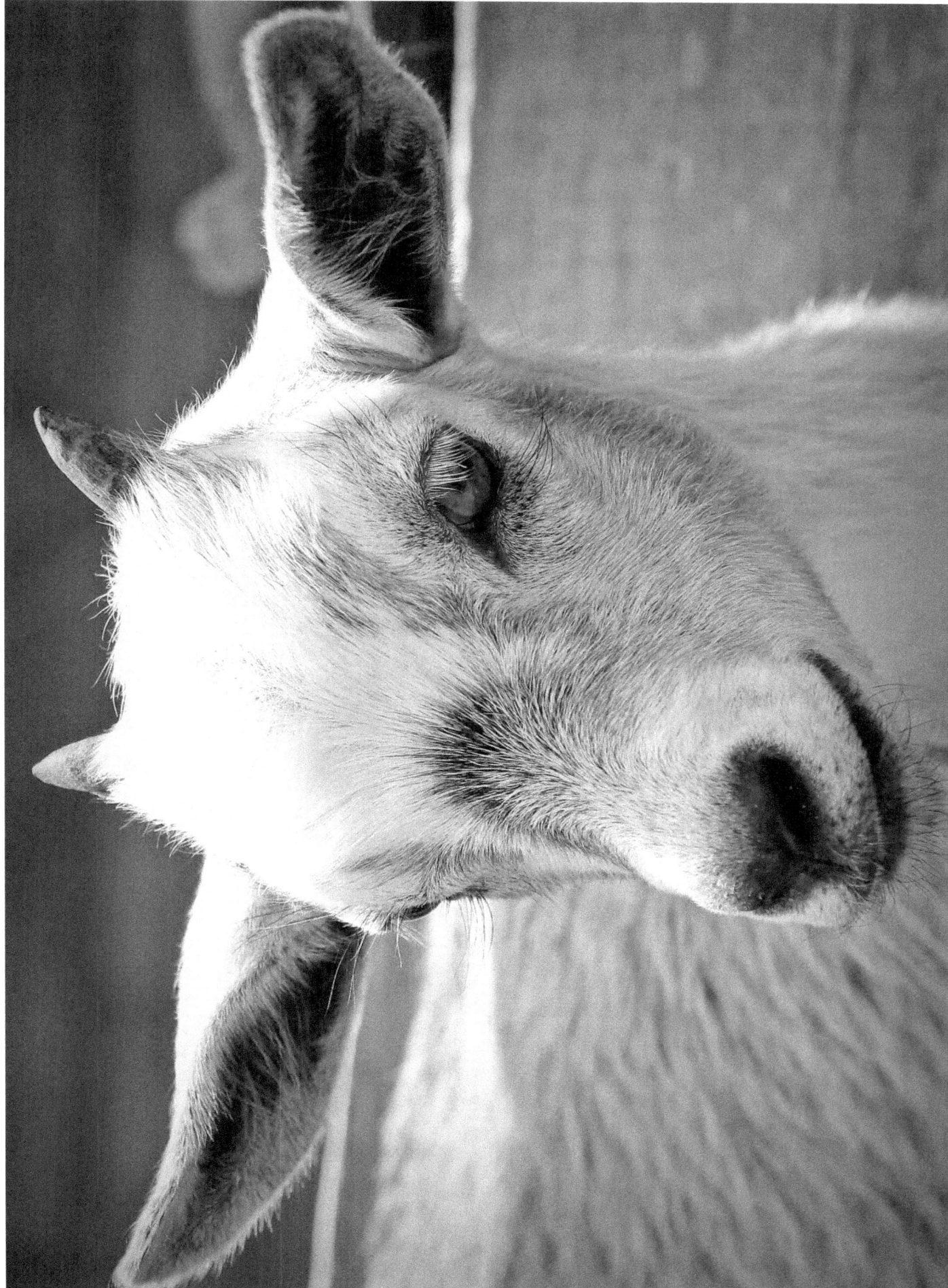

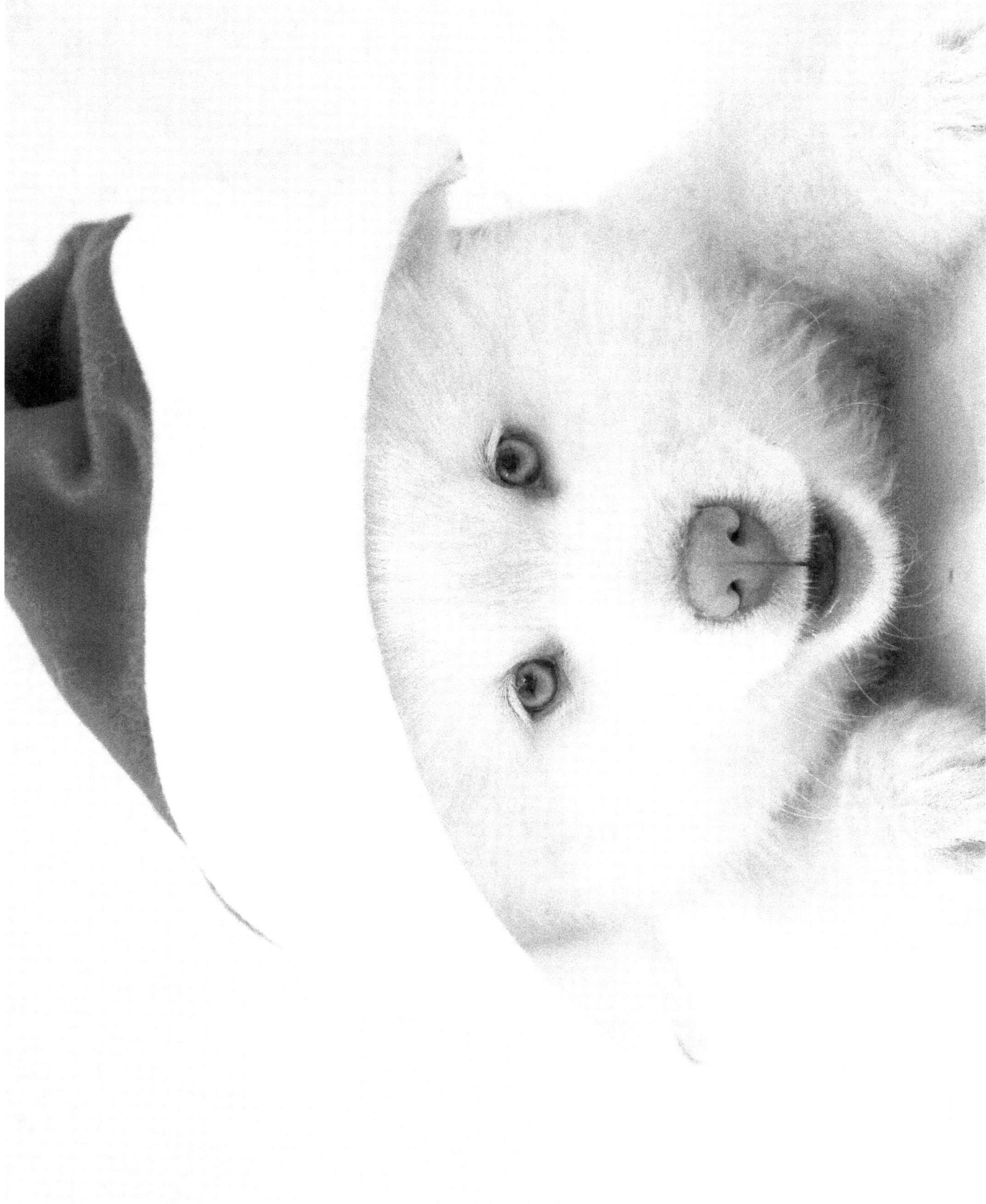

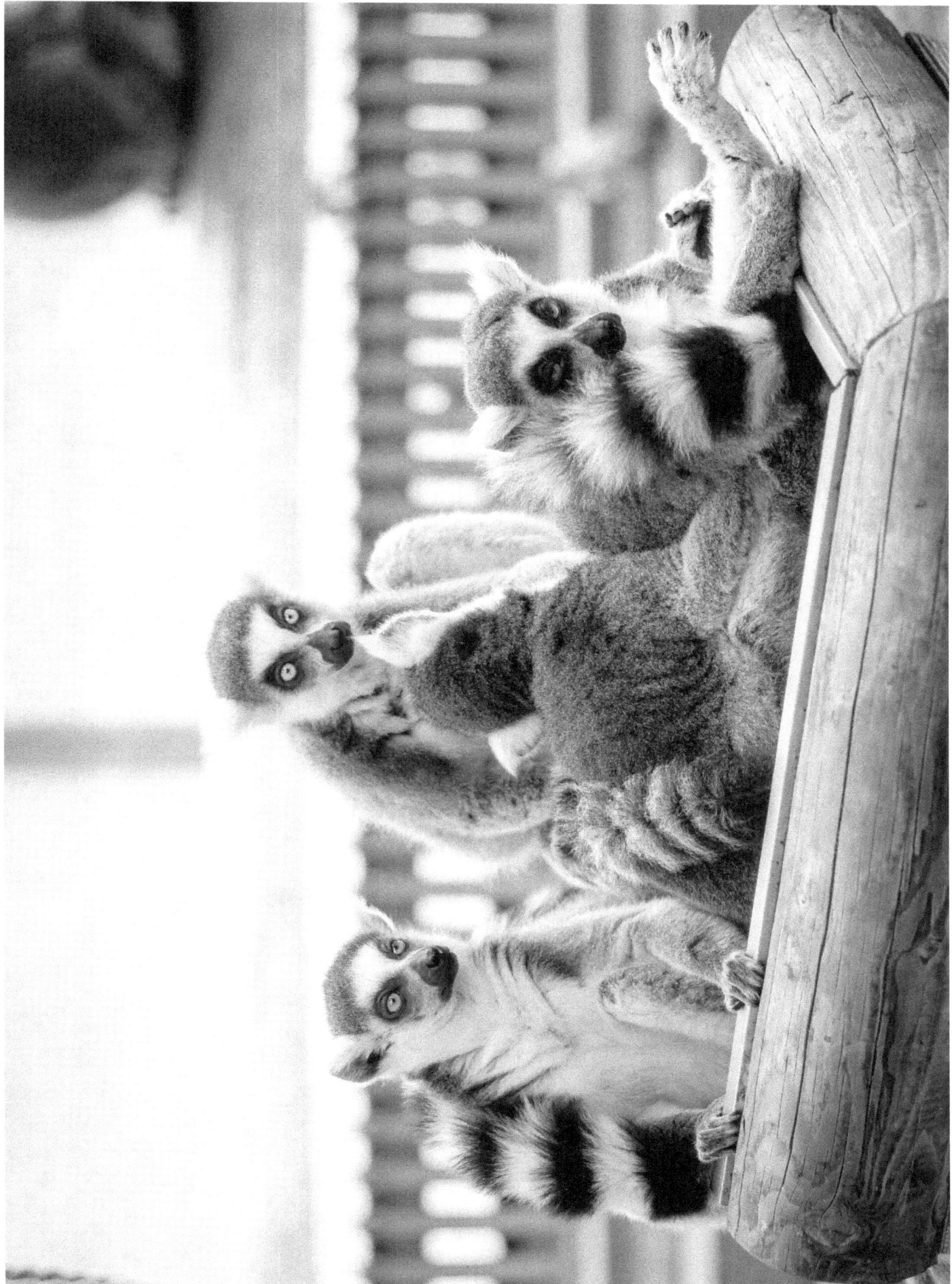

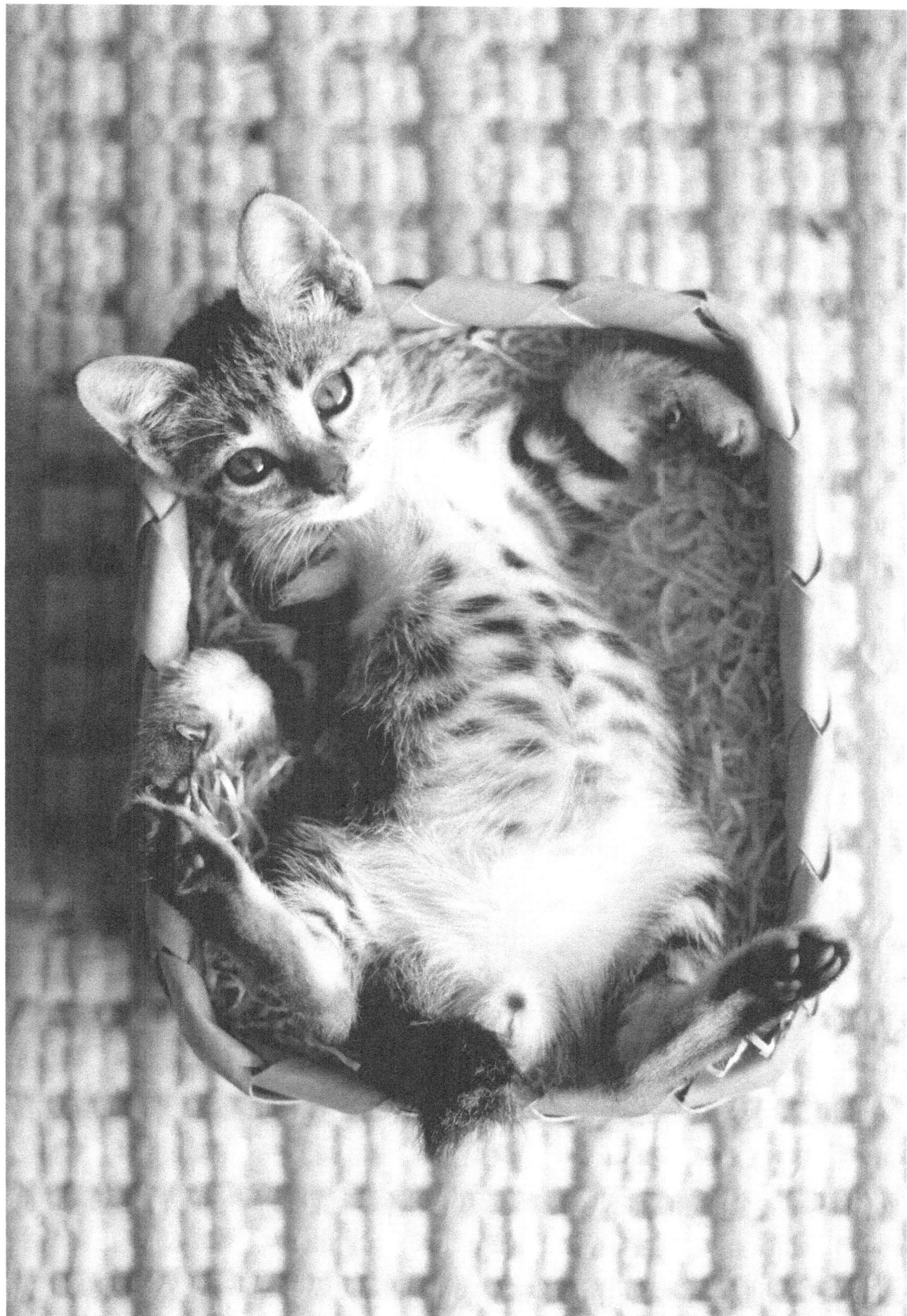

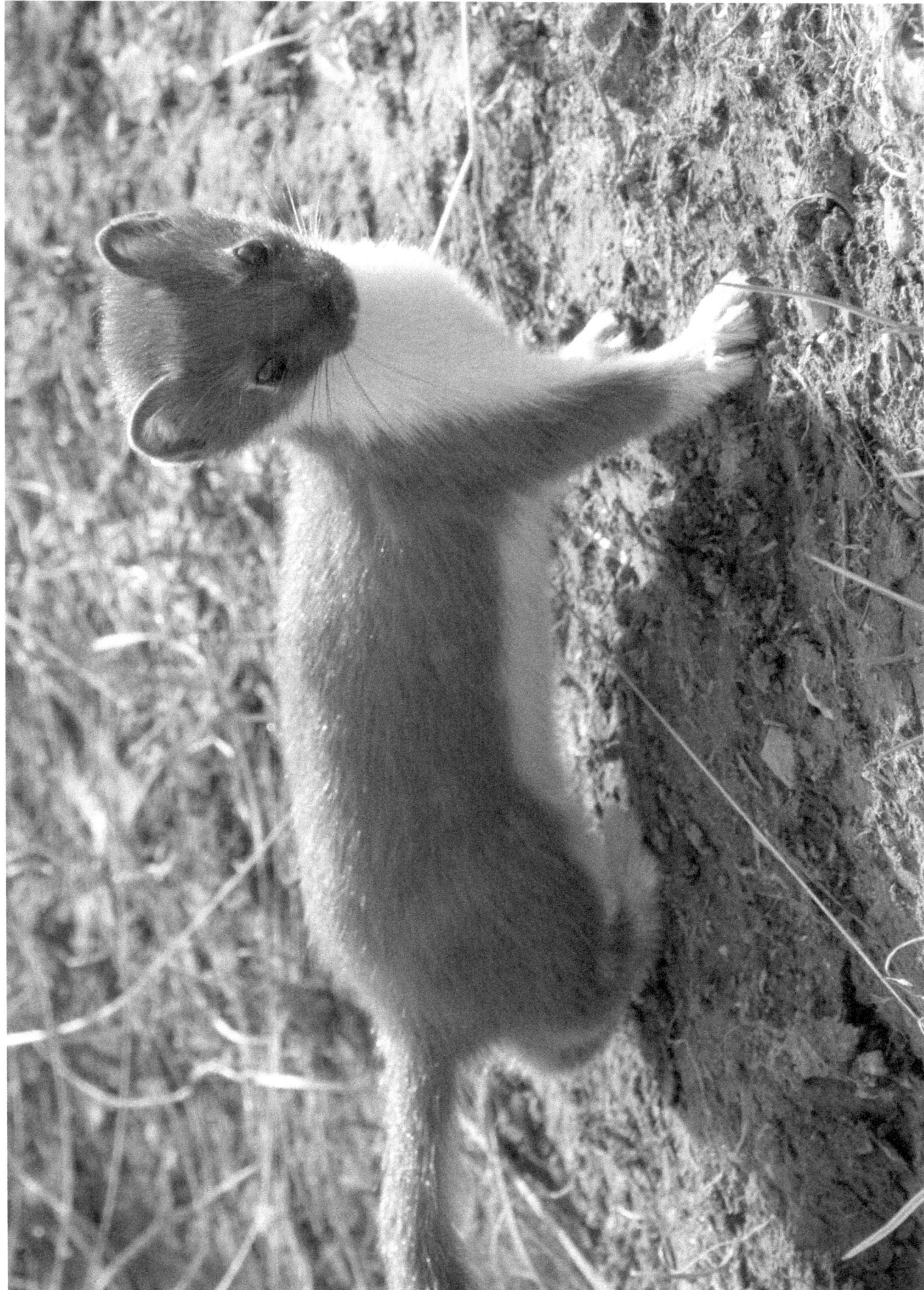

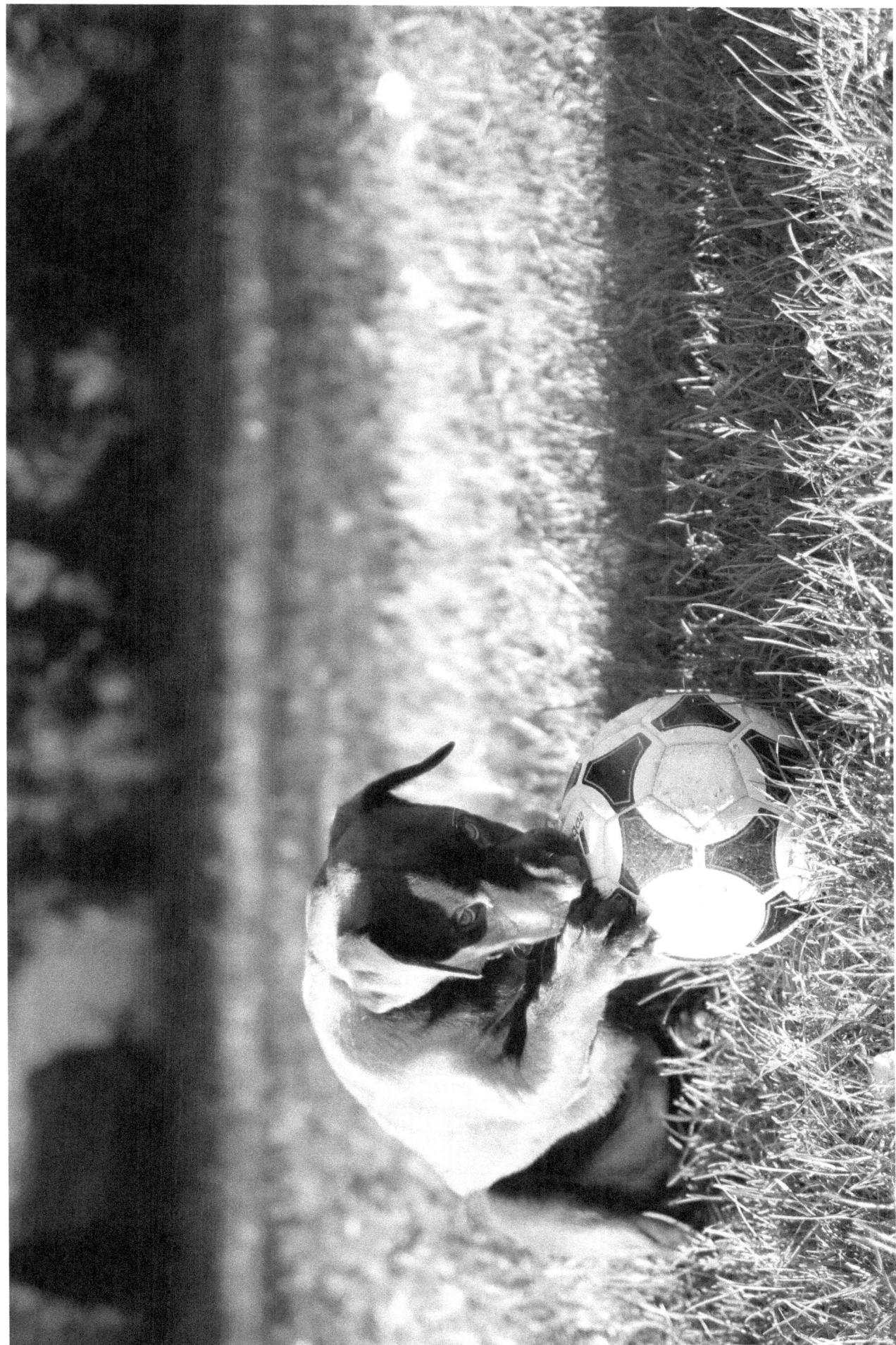

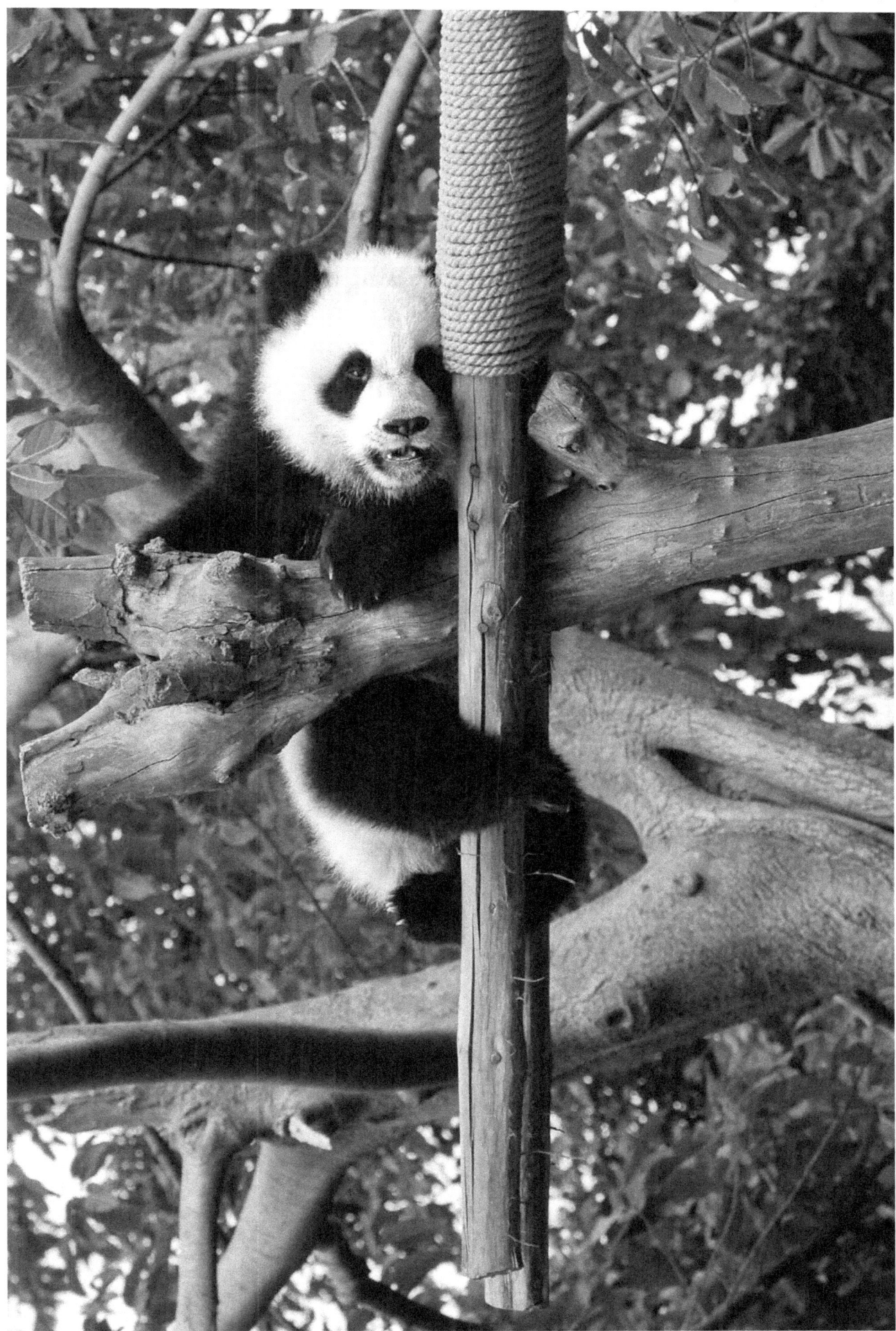

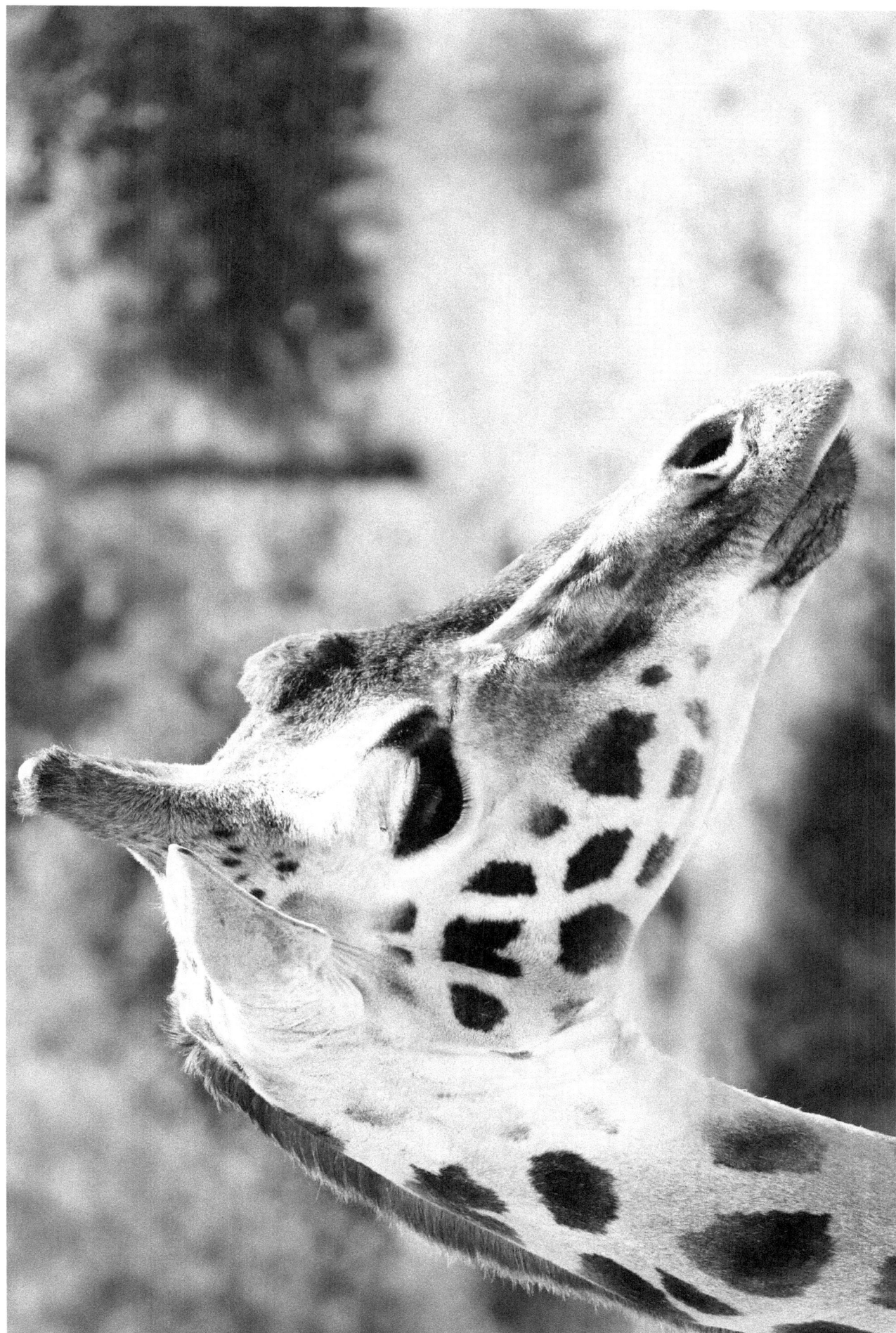

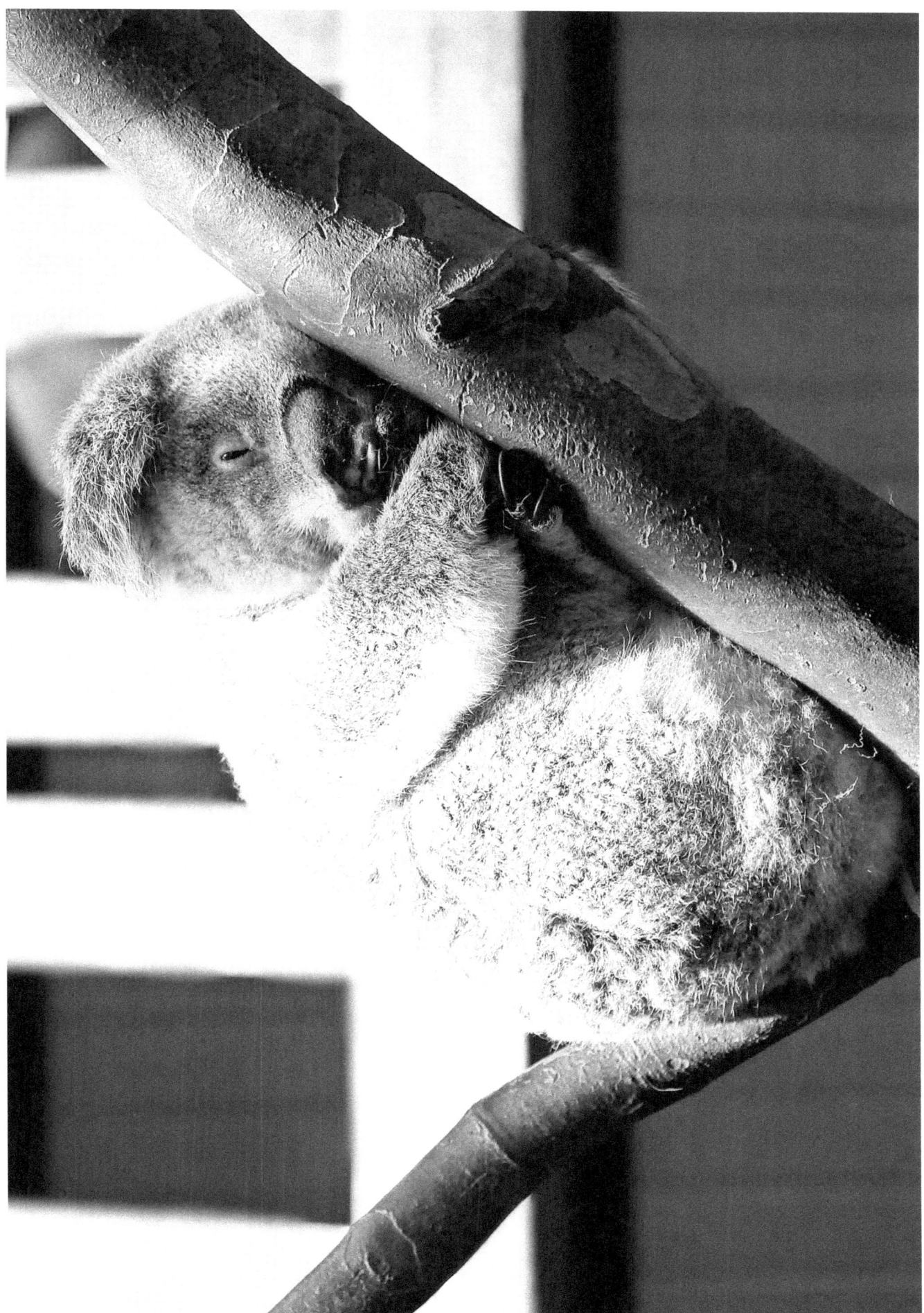

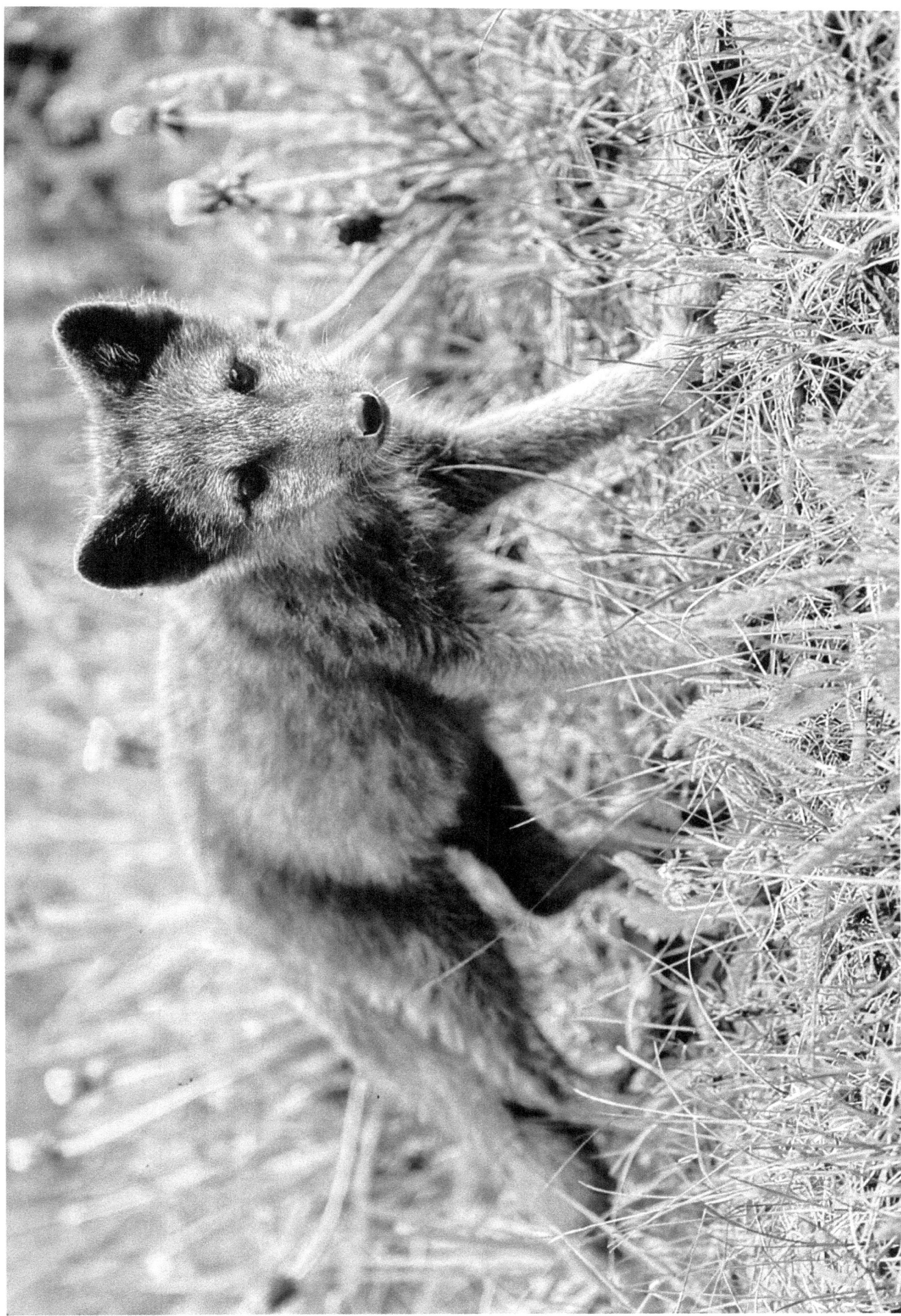

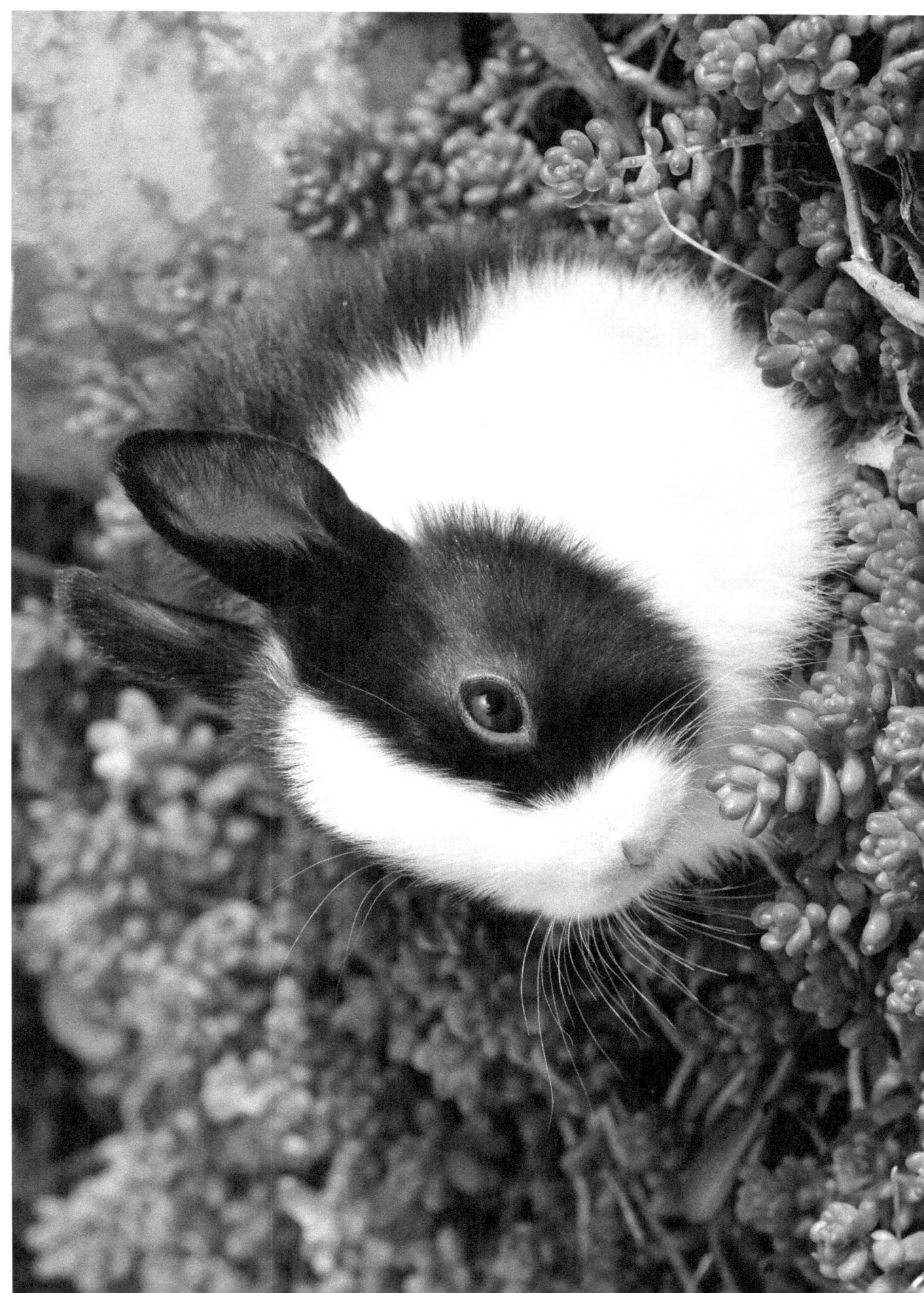

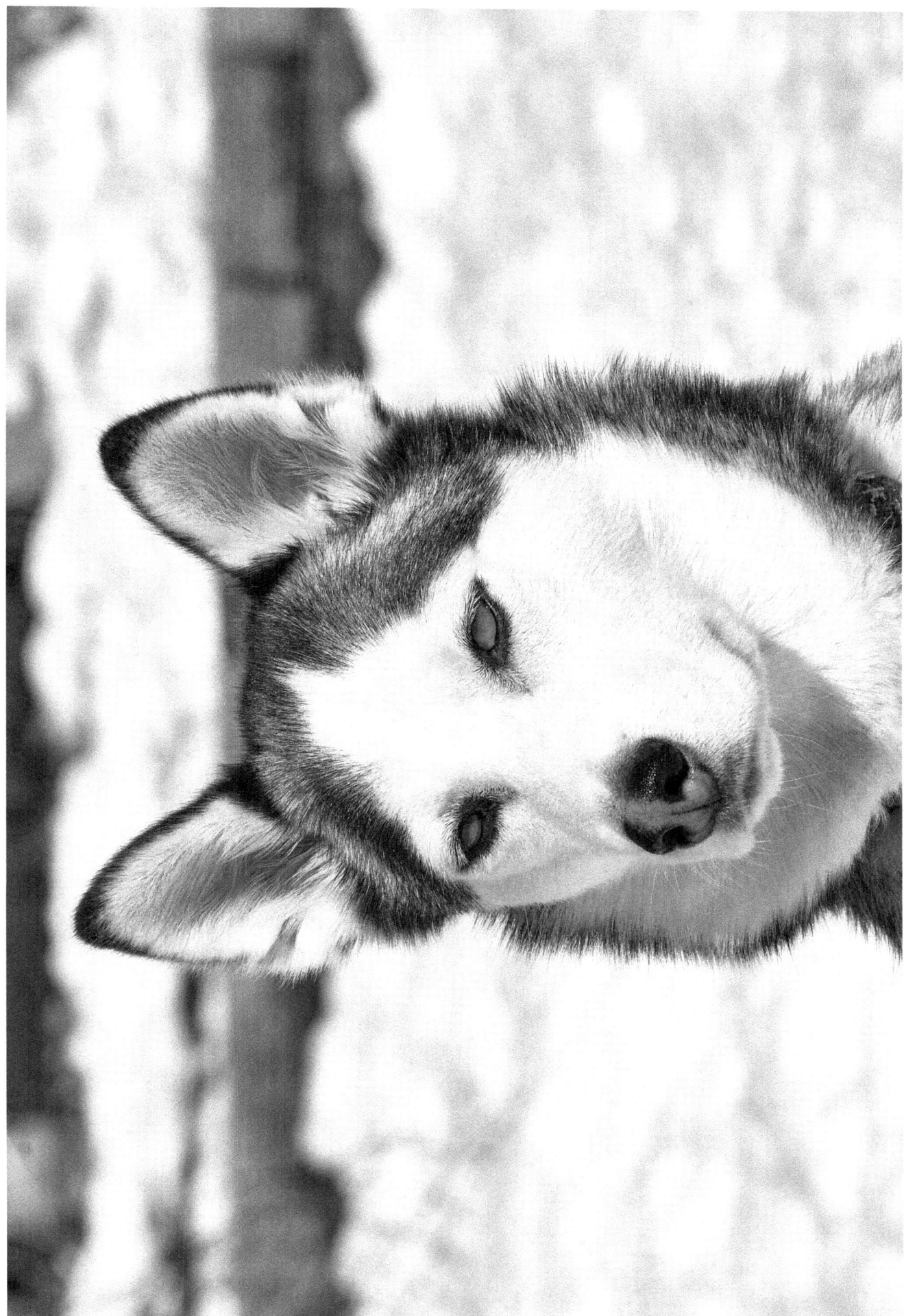

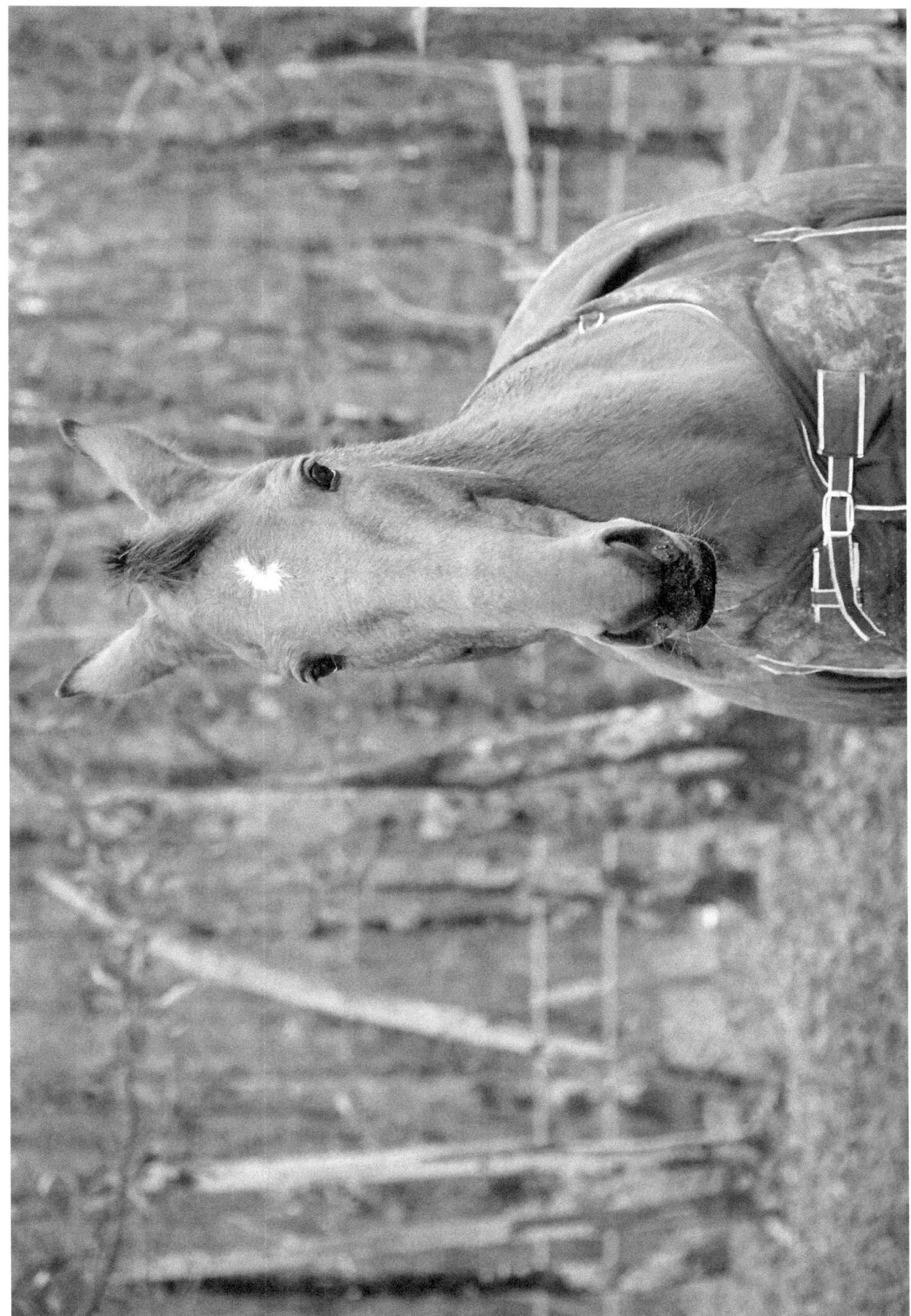

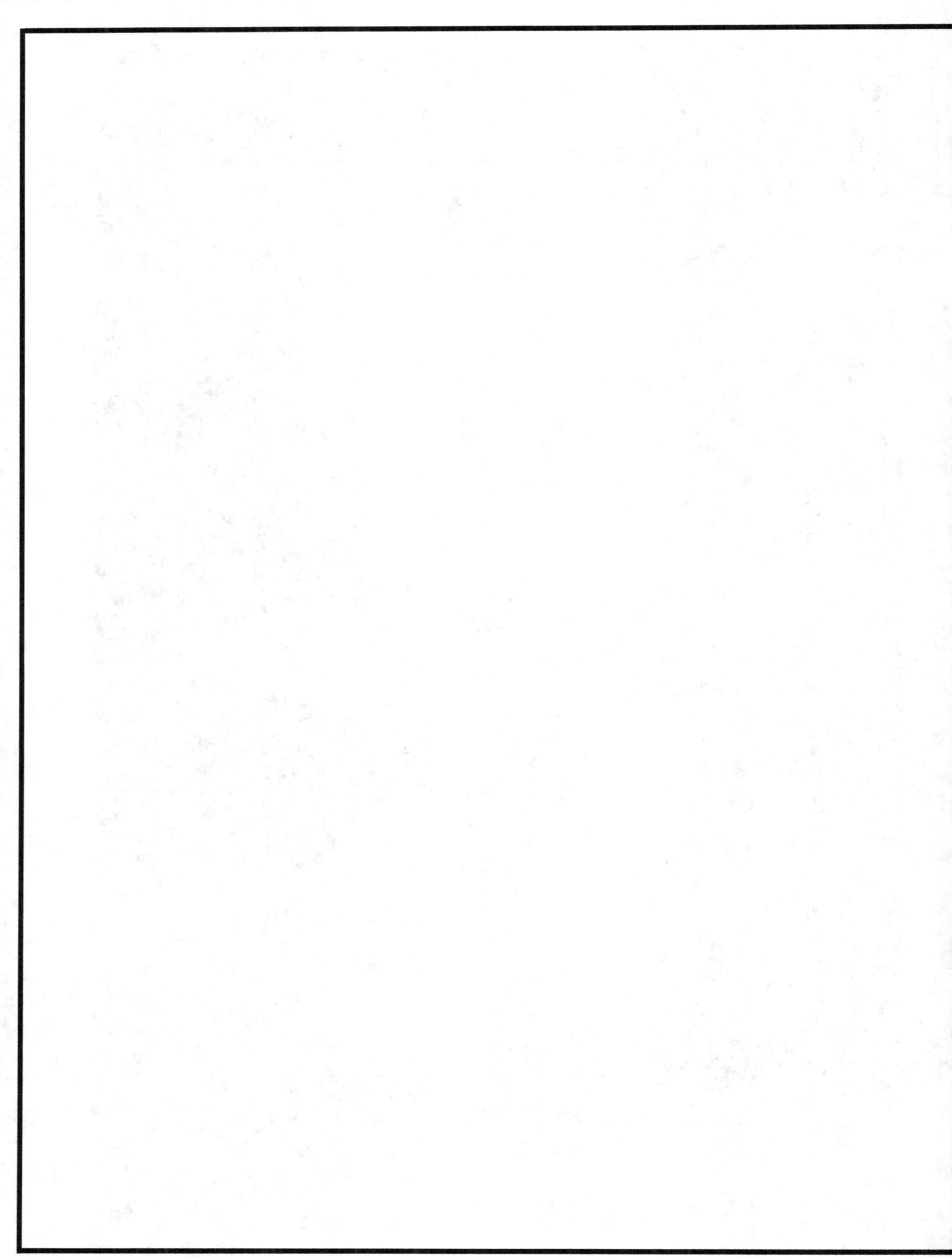

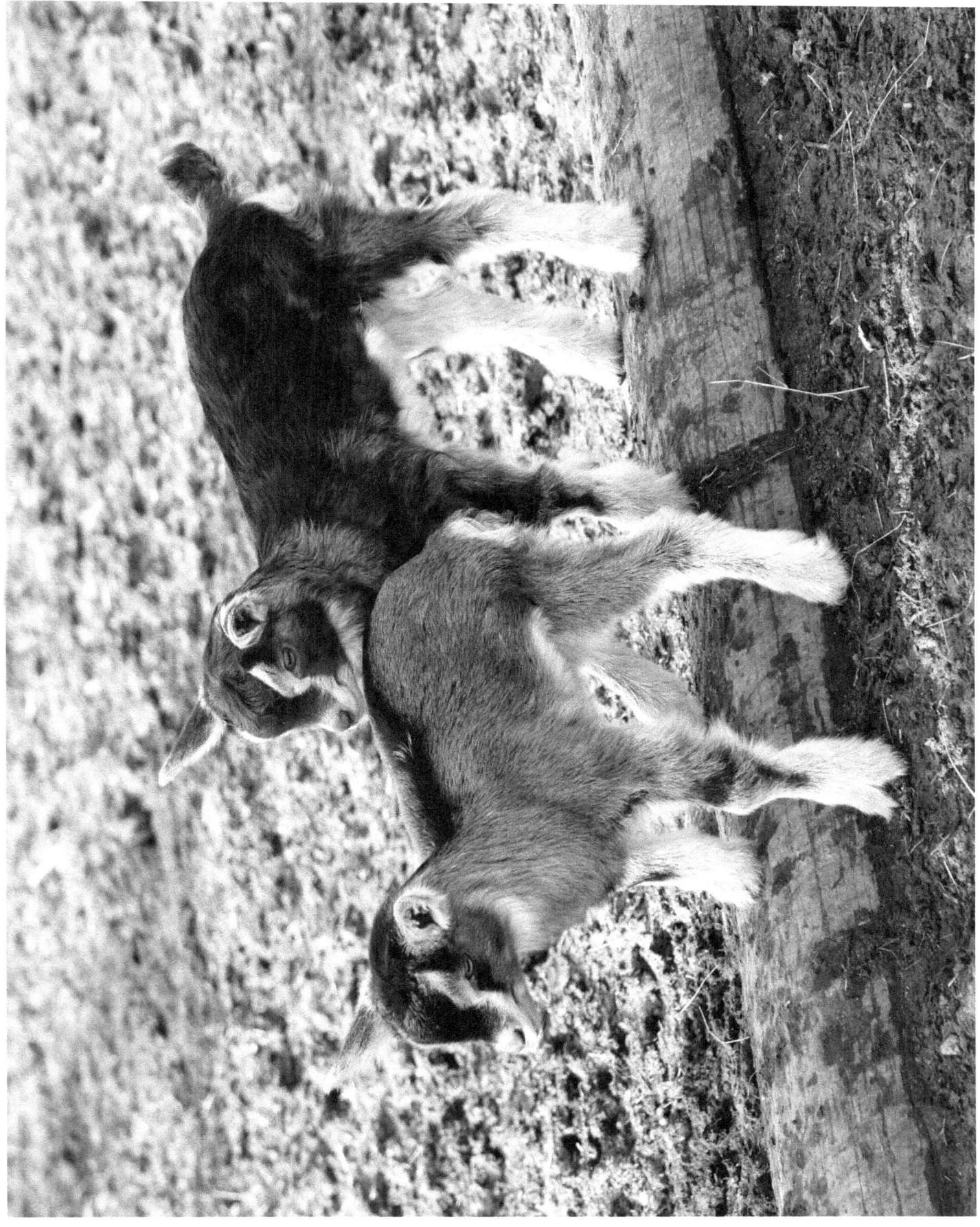

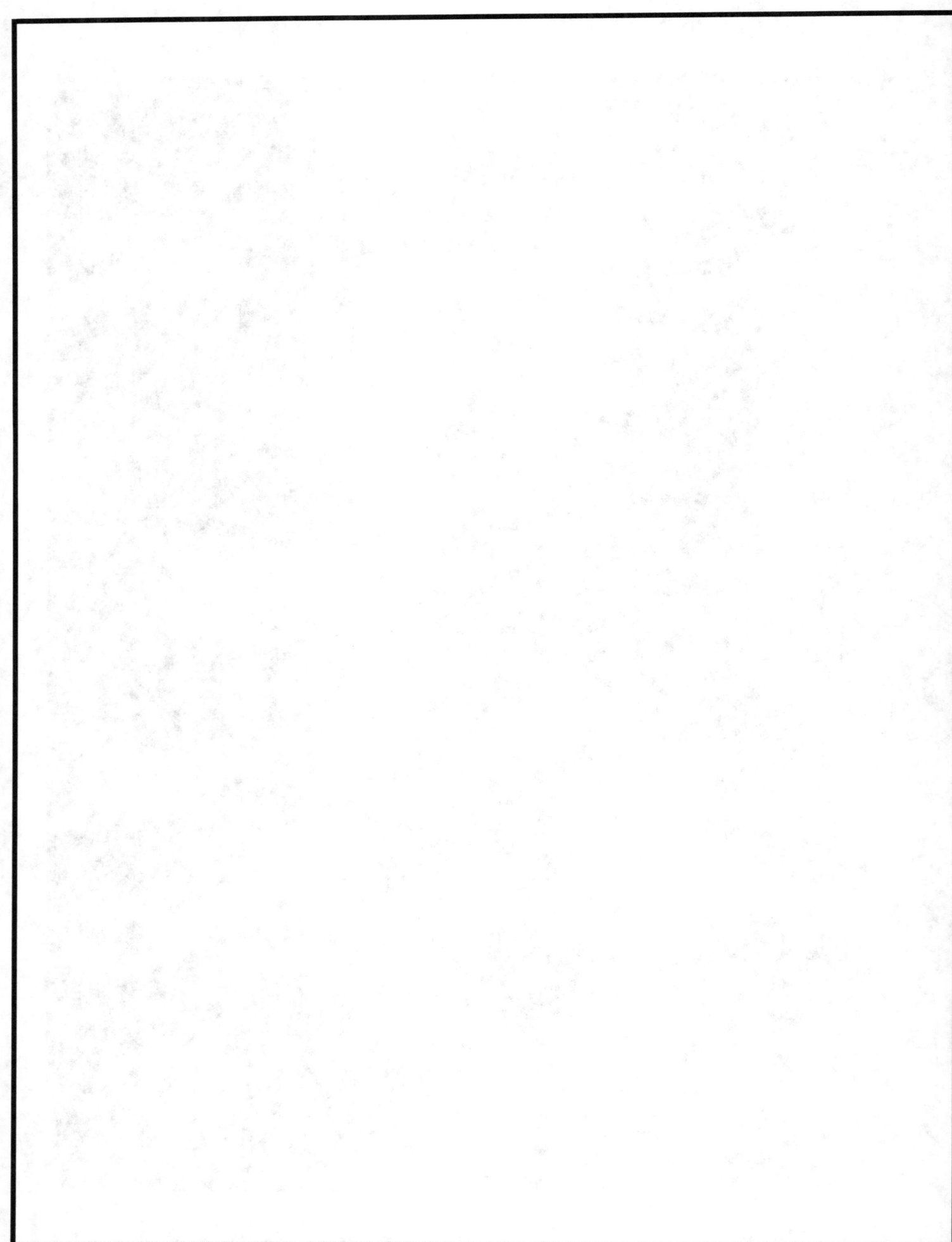

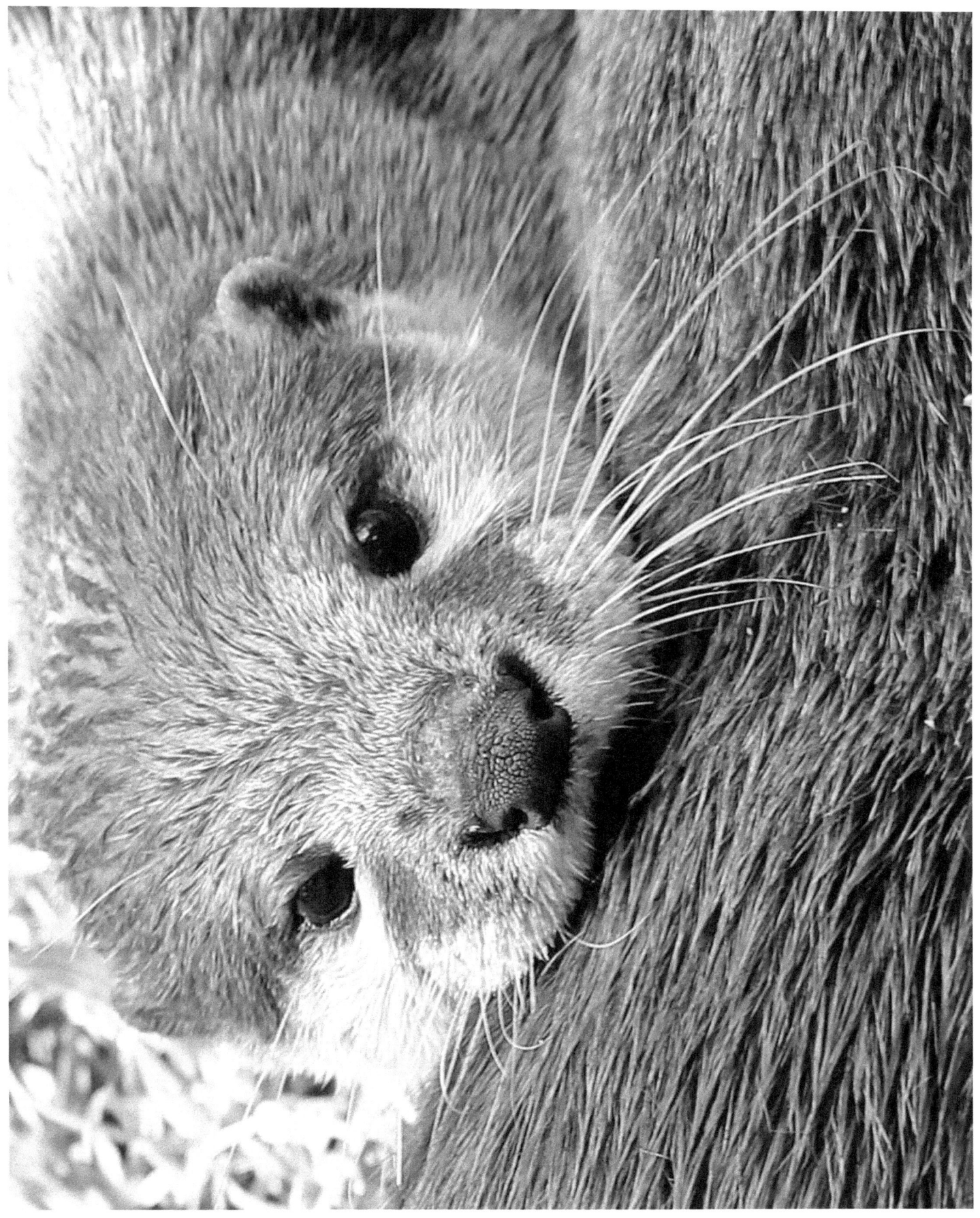

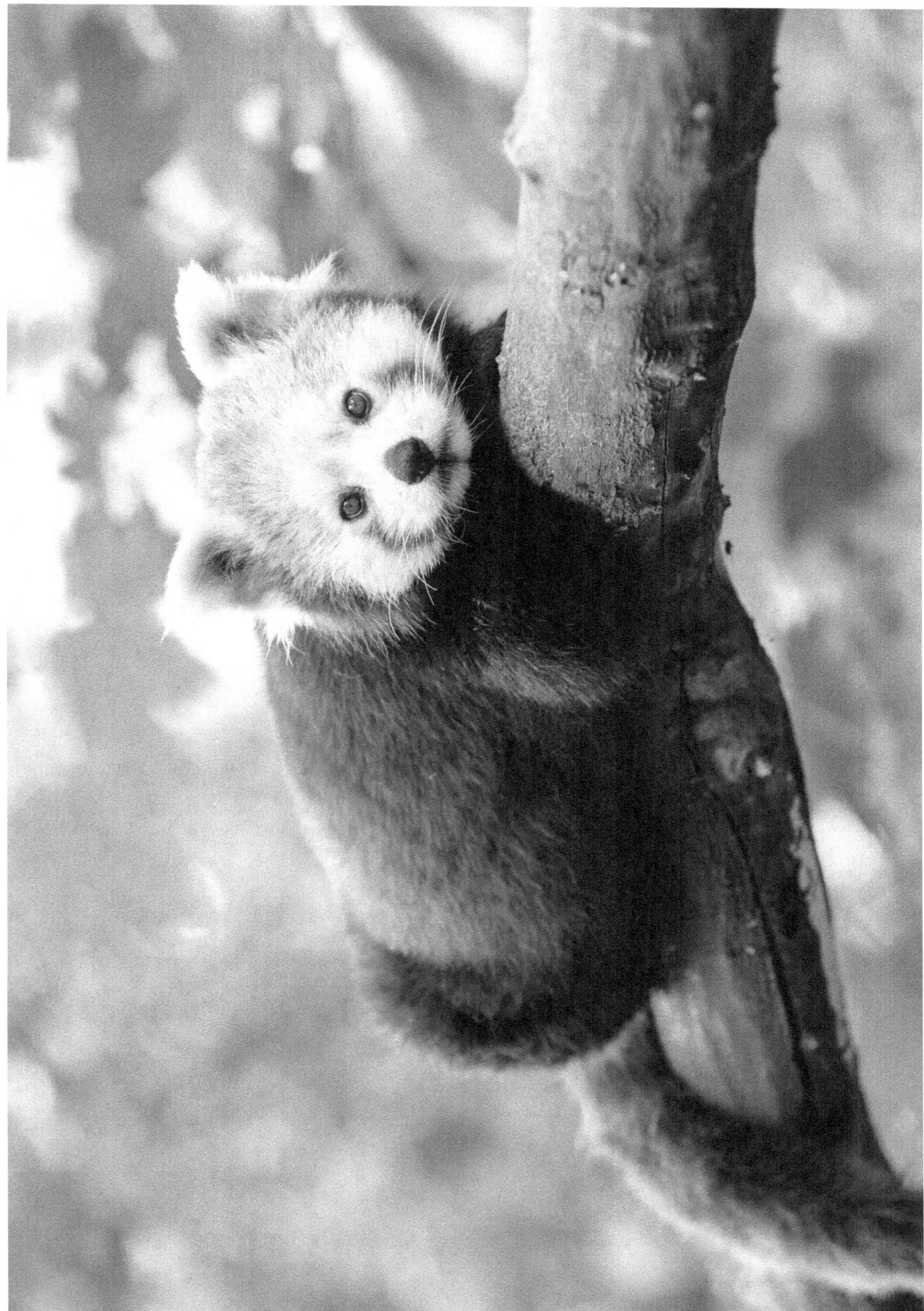

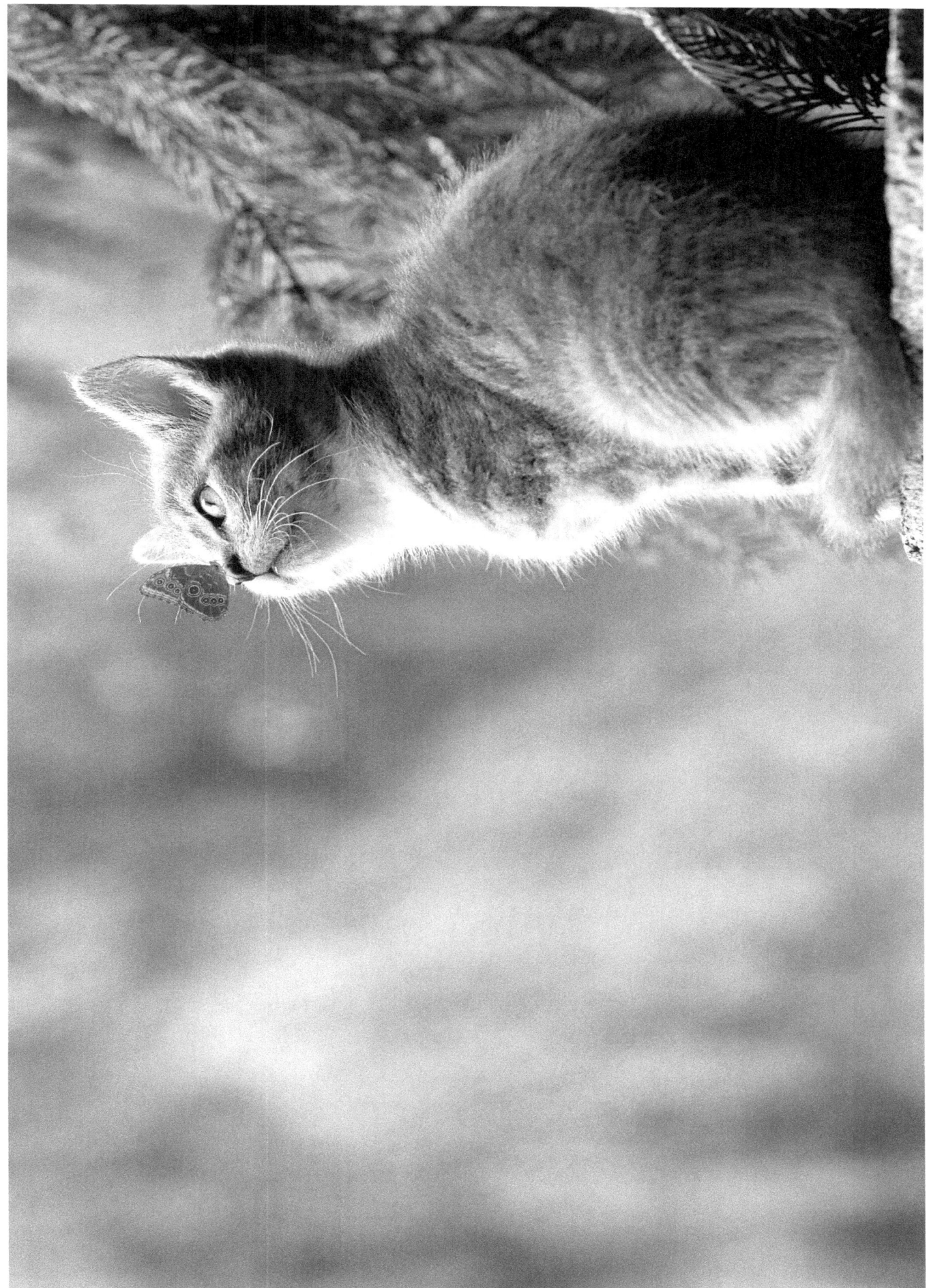

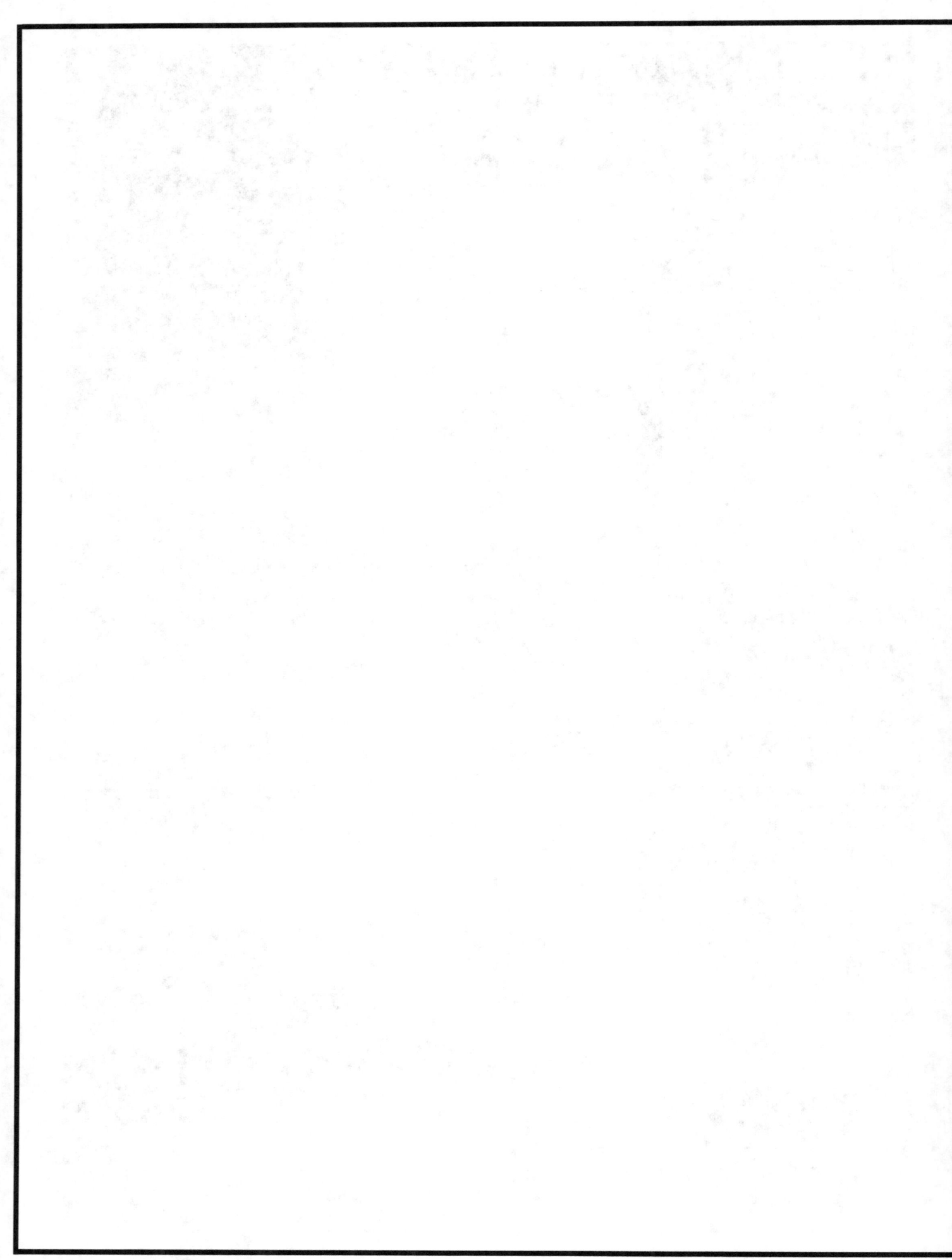

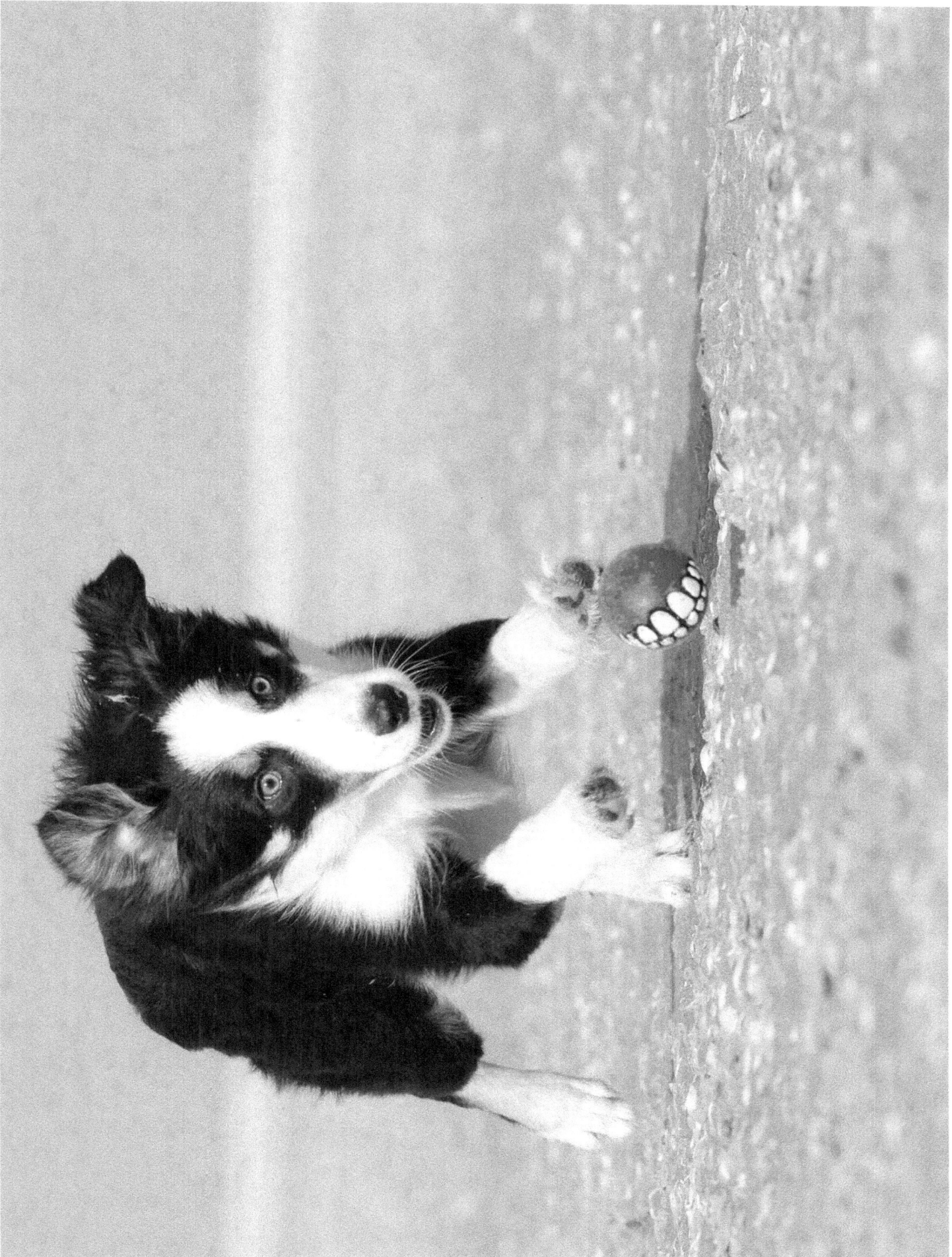

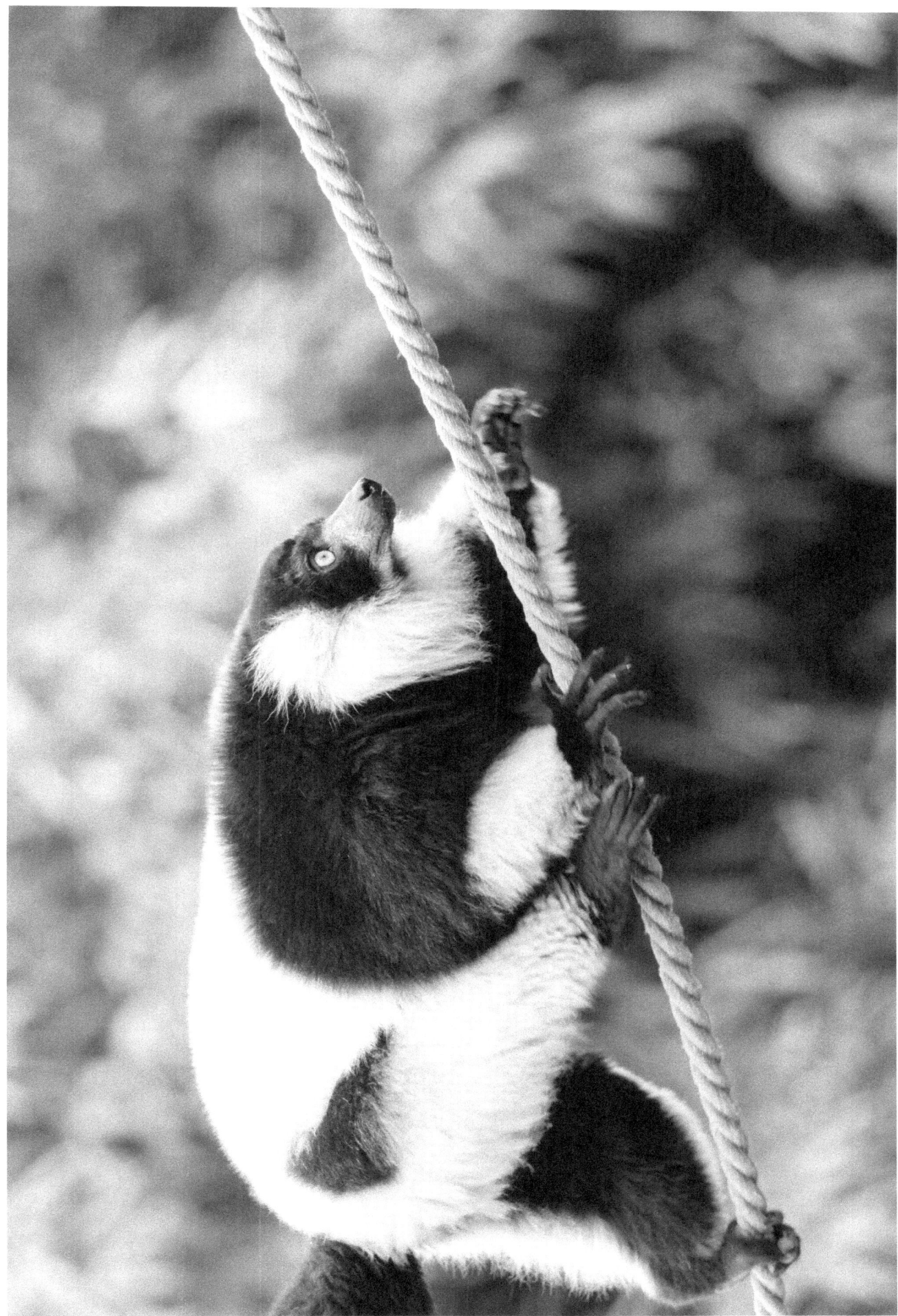

www.ingramcontent.com/pod-product-compliance
Lightning Source LLC
Chambersburg PA
CBHW080909220526
45466CB00011BA/3520